The School For Wives

Molière's
The School for Wives

A New Version in English by
Frédérique Michel &
Charles A. Duncombe

CITY GARAGE   LOS ANGELES

Cover Design by: Paul M. Rubenstein

Cover Photo: Jessica Madison, Bo Roberts in *The School for Wives,* City Garage, 2009.

Note

This is not an academic translation. We wanted to do our own version for our company at City Garage in order to better capture the language and spirit of Molière. We hope you will enjoy it as much as the audience did. We decided to publish our series of French classic comedies in case other companies might find them useful.

Acknowledgments

The authors would like to express their gratitude to the people who put together this book: Freddy J. Nager and his company Atomic Tango for their publishing expertise, Cynthia Mance for her careful copyediting, Paul Rubenstein for his photography and cover design... and to also thank them for their loyalty and friendship.

This version of *The School for Wives* was first performed at City Garage in Los Angeles in 2009. It was directed by Frédérique Michel and designed by Charles A. Duncombe.

In the original production, the roles were played by these actors:

ARNOLPHE	Bo Roberts
AGNES	Jessica Madison
HORACE	Dave Mack
ALAIN	Kenneth Rudnicki
GEORGETTE	Cynthia Mance
CHRYSALDE	David E. Frank
HENRI[*]	Trace Taylor
ORONTE	Jeff Atik
Also:	Troy Dunn
	Michael Galvin
A NOTARY	David E. Frank

Scene
A square in a provincial city

Time
In a time when such things happen

---

[*] In our production, the role was played as "Henriette."

ACT I

Scene 1

ARNOLPHE, CHRYSALDE.

CHRYSALDE
I can't believe what I'm hearing. So you're determined to marry this girl?

ARNOLPHE
Tomorrow. A few days more and she'll be mine.

CHRYSALDE
Then I'd better seize this chance to tell you what I think. I must speak bluntly, as your friend. For any man to take a wife is a risk, but for you, it is courting disaster.

ARNOLPHE
That's your worthy opinion, is it? Might it be, dear friend, that your fears for me are based on your own sad case? You took the gamble yourself and perhaps your wife has lost your wager for you. Otherwise, why such grave concern for me? Has she been letting some feathered fellow tickle her fancy?

CHRYSALDE
I don't believe so. If she has, I'm not aware of it.

ARNOLPHE
But you will be soon enough. Let me feel your head. There, the horns are beginning to sprout even as we speak.

CHRYSALDE
Fool I might be, or fool she may make of me, but the bigger fool is he who lives his life in mortal fear of what has not yet happened or may never happen at all. If fate is going to give you horns, horns you shall have, fight it as you may. But he who suffers agonies over that which, in the end, may not be so very terrible simply turns misfortune into calamity, and over what?

ARNOLPHE
Over what? There speaks a man who's already comfortable as a laughingstock and is looking for company.

CHRYSALDE
This is what concerns me, and why it is more dangerous for you to marry than any man in France.

ARNOLPHE
Absurd.

CHRYSALDE
Is it? All your life you've heaped scorn on every luckless husband you hear about. Nothing gives you

more delight than to mock and gloat over the wretch, whether the poor man is to be blamed or not.

ARNOLPHE
And why shouldn't I sneer? Is there a town in France with men more willing to suffer such indignities?

CHRYSALDE
Oh, come now. It's not as bad as all that.

ARNOLPHE
Is it not? Look around you. Here's a man who's busy making a fortune. There's his wife, busy spreading the wealth, but not in the way he thinks. Here's another, pleased with the lavish gifts his wife receives, proud to see, as she explains to him, all these tributes to her purity. Another, overcome by his suspicions, storms and rants and what does that get him? She claims that life with such a brute is unendurable and he deserves anything he gets.

CHRYSALDE
But this is too much.

ARNOLPHE
Not at all. Look here, one has a clever wife who seems to make him her greatest confidant, complaining of the crowd of young men who never cease to annoy her. He, more the fool, pities them for their vain efforts—efforts that are far from unsuccessful. Look there, a man's wife explains that

her new jewels are the result of good luck at cards while he, never guessing what kind of game she's really playing, offers his congratulation. But worst of all is the one who simply resigns himself and, when his wife's lovers come to call, politely welcomes them, takes his own hat, and meekly creeps away. With such laughable examples all around, how should I not ridicule them all?

CHRYSALDE
This is exactly why I fear for you. Those you mock may one day be mocking you. For my part, I find no joy in other men's grief. I hold my tongue and am grateful to avoid their fate. But if I don't, and become a laughingstock, as you say, I hope that others will look kindly on me, even feel sympathy for my bad luck. But not so with you. With your cruel wit and merciless jokes, if the least whisper was ever heard about your wife, why they'd crow about your misfortune from the housetops.

ARNOLPHE
Don't waste your worry on me, my friend. I know very well how to take care of my affairs. Believe me, they'll get no chance to jeer at me. I know all the little tricks wives use to deceive their husbands. That's why I've secured my peace of mind forever by taking to wife a girl who is completely innocent, untouched by the evil influence of the world.

CHRYSALDE
They all start out like that.

ARNOLPHE
But I've taken steps to insure she remains that way.
She's not only pure, she's as stupid as can be.

CHRYSALDE
And is this something to brag about? Is ignorance
such a virtue?

ARNOLPHE
It is. I'm proud to say she knows nothing at all.
Everything that she learns she will learn from me.

CHRYSALDE
Are you to be her husband or her schoolmaster?

ARNOLPHE
Both. I will conduct my household as a School For
Wives, and when she completes her education, there
will be no more perfect wife than she. I've even
written a text for her to learn by heart. A man's not
stupid to take a stupid wife. Yours, no doubt, is wise
enough, and therein lies the risk. Marry a woman
with too many brains and you're bound to suffer. I'll
have no intellectual, holding her salons, inviting the
young wits, while I, the dull husband, stand around
looking after their coats. No, keep the smart ones.
They know too much for their own good—or mine. I
want an unaccomplished wife. There are only three

things I want her to know how to do: pray, sew, and love me above all else.

CHRYSALDE
But what a bore it sounds! A wife so stupid.

ARNOLPHE
I'd rather have stupidity that I can trust than intelligence I fear.

CHRYSALDE
But wit and beauty...

ARNOLPHE
Virtue is enough for me.

CHRYSALDE
But how can an idiot know what's virtuous? How dull to have such an empty-headed wife. And what, pray, makes her more trustworthy? If a clever woman breaks her vows at least she knows what she's doing. Such a dunce as you describe might commit adultery without even knowing it.

ARNOLPHE
Say what you like, you won't change my mind. I'll have an ignorant bride and that's that.

CHRYSALDE
Then so be it.

ARNOLPHE
Each man has his own strategy for wedded bliss and
I'll follow mine. I'm rich, so I can take a wife who'll
be dependent on me in every way—a sweet,
submissive girl with neither name nor fortune of her
own. I have just the girl in Agnes. From the age of
four her meek expression has enchanted me. From
the moment I first saw her I knew she would one day
make the perfect wife. She was an orphan, being
raised by a peasant woman, who was grateful to turn
her over to my care. I had her raised in a convent, far
from the temptations of the world, and instructed the
nuns strictly in what she was to be taught: exactly
nothing. They have kept her mind a perfect void,
which is just what I wanted, and now, as a grown
young woman, she's in my care at last. I've hidden
her here, in another house I own, and to protect her
purity, I've hired two servants who are as simple-
minded as she. I tell you all this so that you can see
how far in advance I've made my plans. If you want
a perfect wife, you must create her yourself. And, to
convince you completely, I wish you to dine with us
tonight. You can see for yourself whether or not my
joy in the result is justified.

CHRYSALDE
Delighted.

ARNOLPHE
You'll be struck not only by her beauty but
convinced of her modesty and ignorance.

CHRYSALDE
    As to her ignorance, based on what you've said, I
    have little doubt.

ARNOLPHE
    My friend, wait till you hear her. Her utter naiveté
    keeps me in stitches. The things she says. Why, the
    other day she came to me as sincerely as you please
    and asked me with great gravity whether children are
    conceived through the air.

CHRYSALDE
    I'm happy indeed for you, *cher* Monsieur Arnolphe.

ARNOLPHE
    Good God, why must you insist on using my former
    name?

CHRYSALDE
    I'm used to it, I suppose. Really, "de la Souche" is
    such an odd choice. What got into you to re-baptize
    yourself at your age? And what, in honor of a tree
    stump at your place in the country?

ARNOLPHE
    It goes with the property. And it sounds much better
    to me. More refined.

CHRYSALDE
    But why forsake your father's name for a whimsy
    like that? I admit it's all the rage just now, but I don't
    see it. Why, the other day I heard tell of a peasant

named Gros Pierre who had a little scrap of land,
perhaps half an acre, dug a ditch around it and
renamed himself Monsieur de l'Isle.

ARNOLPHE
Thanks for the commentary, but my name's de la
Souche, and I'll thank you to address me that way.

CHRYSALDE
It's not catching on very fast. I've seen that most of
your mail still comes addressed to your former self.

ARNOLPHE
I can accept that from those who are still learning of
the change, but from you...

CHRYSALDE
Enough scolding. From now on, it will be "Good
day, Monsieur de la Souche."

ARNOLPHE
Excellent. And now I'll bid you farewell until
tonight. I'll just knock and let them know I'm back in
town at last.

CHRYSALDE
Until tonight. *Aside.* The man's a lunatic. Quite mad.

Exit, CHRYSALDE.

ARNOLPHE
Alone. He's crazy, poor fellow. Can't see sense. No

doubt it comes from worrying night and day about what his wife is up to.

He knocks.

ARNOLPHE
Hey! Hey there! *Aside.* They'll be so happy to see me after being away for an entire ten days.

Scene 2

ARNOLPHE, GEORGETTE, ALAIN.

ALAIN
    Who's there?

ARNOLPHE
    I am!

ALAIN
    Who?

ARNOLPHE
    Me.

ALAIN
    Me?

ARNOLPHE
    Yes!

ALAIN
    No, you're wrong. I'm not there. I'm here.

ARNOLPHE
    Not you. Me. I'm here.

ALAIN
    No, you're not. I'm here. And you're there.

ARNOLPHE
Not you, me! Me!

ALAIN
That's what I said. Georgette!

GEORGETTE
What?

ARNOLPHE
Open up, you blockhead!

ALAIN
There's some poor half-wit at the door.

GEORGETTE
Who is it?

ALAIN
He says it's me, but I think he's mistaken.

GEORGETTE
If it's a half-wit it must be you.

ARNOLPHE
Let me in!

GEORGETTE
Is that him doing all the shouting?

ALAIN
He says it's me.

GEORGETTE
Well, what are you shouting about?

ALAIN
He says I want to come in.

GEORGETTE
That's stupid. You're already in.

ARNOLPHE
Open up you idiots!

ALAIN
There he goes again. I think you'd better get the door.

GEORGETTE
He sounds like a crazy person. Or maybe a burglar.

ARNOLPHE
Open up! Open up!

GEORGETTE
Why is he pretending to be you?

ALAIN
Maybe it's a disguise to fool us.

GEORGETTE
I'm not letting him in. You know the master said we shouldn't let anyone in.

ARNOLPHE
    I am your master!

GEORGETTE
    Now he says *he's* the master.

ALAIN
    I wish he'd make up his mind.

GEORGETTE
    How do we know it's him?

ARNOLPHE
    You rotten harlot!

ALAIN
    Sounds like him.

ARNOLPHE
    Open up, you ass!

GEORGETTE
    He recognized you, too.

ARNOLPHE
    If one of you doesn't open this door this instant
    you'll get nothing but bread and water for three days!

GEORGETTE
    He says he's going to starve us. That's the master, all
    right.

ALAIN
Then let's definitely not let him in.

ARNOLPHE
Open up! Open up! Open up!

ALAIN
I think you'd better get the door.

ARNOLPHE
Whoever opens this door is going to be beaten until
they can't see straight!

GEORGETTE
You get it.

ARNOLPHE
That's what I get for hiring two idiots.

ALAIN
We'd better both go. Let's do it together, then run.

GEORGETTE
Good idea. That way if it really is a burglar, we can
hide until he's gone.

*They open the door, try to run. ARNOLPHE snatches
them both.*

ARNOLPHE
Idiots! What do you think you're doing?

ALAIN
  Nothing!

ARNOLPHE
  Exactly. Why didn't you let me in?

ALAIN
  You said you were me but I was already inside.

ARNOLPHE
  Beating him. Blast you!

ALAIN
  It's her fault too, sir!

GEORGETTE
  Not me! I said not to open on account you were a
  burglar.

ARNOLPHE
  And if I was?

GEORGETTE
  We would have hid!

ARNOLPHE
  Leaving my house in the keeping of these two. What
  was I thinking? All right, all right, enough of this
  nonsense. I wish to see my ward, Agnes. *To Alain.*
  Go fetch her.

Exit, ALAIN.

ARNOLPHE
To Georgette. Tell me, how is she? Was she unhappy while I was out of town?

GEORGETTE
Unhappy? Of course not.

ARNOLPHE
What do you mean?

GEORGETTE
Why should she be unhappy?

ARNOLPHE
Because I was away, of course.

GEORGETTE
Oh that. No, she wasn't unhappy at all.

ARNOLPHE
Why not?

GEORGETTE
Because she was always thinking you had already come back again. Every time a donkey, mule, or ass passed in the street she was sure it was you.

Enter AGNES, ALAIN.

Scene 3

ARNOLPHE, AGNES, ALAIN, GEORGETTE.

ARNOLPHE
She has her sewing with her. That's a good sign. *To AGNES.* Well, dear Agnes you see I'm back at last. Are you glad to see me?

AGNES
Oh yes, sir.

ARNOLPHE
I'm glad to see you too. Is everything all right, my dear?

AGNES
Oh yes. Except for the mouse.

ARNOLPHE
A mouse?

AGNES
Last night in my room. And what mischief he got up to!

ARNOLPHE
Well, don't fear. Very soon there will be someone to drive little mousey away. Now then, what are you making?

AGNES
A lace handkerchief.

ARNOLPHE
What fine work. How cunning your little hands and
to what good use they will soon be set.

AGNES
What use is that, uncle?

ARNOLPHE
All in good time, sweet girl. And what about my
nightshirts?

AGNES
They're all finished, uncle.

ARNOLPHE
Now, now, you don't need to call me uncle anymore.
That was just a formality when I took you under my
care. We're not really family, you see, not actually
related.

AGNES
Are we not?

ARNOLPHE
Why, no indeed. You seem disappointed.

AGNES
Oh, but I am! *Embracing him.* You're my only
family in the entire world. Or so I thought.

ARNOLPHE
Gently freeing himself. Have no concern, my dear. We'll be family soon enough.

AGNES
And how is that to be, since you just said that we are not related?

ARNOLPHE
Don't strain to understand. You go along upstairs. I'll come back and see you shortly. We'll have a serious talk and everything will be clear.

AGNES
That will make me very happy.

Exit all but ARNOLPHE.

ARNOLPHE
How adorable she is. And how blessed am I in her ignorance! All the learned ladies in the world, with all their wit and so-called accomplishments, can't compare to the charm and goodness of this modest innocent. What matters that she has no dowry? What's money to me when such a treasure is to be mine!

Enter, HORACE.

Scene 4

ARNOLPHE, HORACE.

HORACE
  Monsieur Arnolphe?

ARNOLPHE
  I beg your pardon, sir, my name is...

HORACE
  It is!

ARNOLPHE
  What's this? Can it be you, my dear friend's son?

HORACE
  Yes, Monsieur, it's me. Horace!

ARNOLPHE
  Horace! I can scarcely believe it.

HORACE
  Monsieur Arnolphe, how glad I am to see you.

ARNOLPHE
  But how long have you been here?

HORACE
  Nine days.

ARNOLPHE
   And yet you never came to see me? What would
   your father think?

HORACE
   No, no. I was anxious to look you up. I called at
   your house more than a week ago.

ARNOLPHE
   Oh, of course. I had some business in the country.

HORACE
   Yes, they'd said you'd gone.

ARNOLPHE
   How quickly children grow up. Why, the last time I
   saw you, you were no more than this high.

HORACE
   Yes indeed, sir, time does go by quickly, as you can
   see.

ARNOLPHE
   But come now, tell me the news of your father, my
   dear friend Oronte. How is the old rascal? Still full
   of mischief? Alas, it's years since we've spoken.

HORACE
   He's very well indeed, still in the peak of health. He
   gave me this note for you, but just today he wrote
   that he is coming here himself. I'm not sure exactly
   why but I think it has something to do with a

merchant friend of yours who went to America some years ago. He's come back filthy rich. Do you know of whom I speak?

ARNOLPHE
No. Did he give a name?

HORACE
Henri, I believe.

ARNOLPHE
No... doesn't ring a bell. I don't think I knew a man of that name.

HORACE
My father writes as if it ought to mean something to me as well, but I'm not sure what. He adds that he and Henri are about to set some enterprise in motion about which he's very vague.

ARNOLPHE
Well, I'll be very happy to see your father after so many years. *Reads note.* But look how he writes. There's no need for such fuss and flattery. Even if he hadn't asked, I would have treated you as a son of my own. How are you fixed? Do you need money?

HORACE
How good you are sir. I confess I am a little short. Could you perhaps advance me as much as a hundred *livres*, do you think?

ARNOLPHE
I'm happy to be of use. Keep the purse. There's at least two hundred there.

HORACE
Allow me to...

ARNOLPHE
No need for pledges and promises. Pay me back when you can. Now, what do you think of our little town. It's not Paris, but it has plenty to offer, does it not?

HORACE
Indeed, sir. Rich in sights and architecture, full of amusements, and, if I may say so, hidden beauties.

ARNOLPHE
Yes, here indeed a man may satisfy his appetites. And if you have a taste for the ladies, you'll find plenty to choose from. They welcome all comers, and their husbands don't appear to mind in the least. You wouldn't believe the little comedies you see played every day. But surely you've discovered that for yourself already, a handsome young lad like you. I'll bet you've already found your way into many a bedroom. Have you no conquests to brag about?

HORACE
Well, since you ask, I'll confess my secret. There is a lady.

ARNOLPHE
Oh good! Another story to add to my repertoire!

HORACE
Sir, I beg you not to reveal my affair to anyone.

ARNOLPHE
Your secret is safe with me. *Aside.* For now.

HORACE
Thank you, sir. As you know, in these delicate matters a single word can shatter all one's hopes. To be plain then, my heart has been stolen by an exquisite creature living nearby. My overtures have been well-received, and not to boast, or to sully her faultless reputation, but I think, sir, that I may hope to soon be rewarded with her love.

ARNOLPHE
Laughing. No doubt you shall. Tell me, who is she?

HORACE
Oh sir, a beauty beyond words. She's the most innocent girl you've ever met, and all because some blind fool has tried to conceal her from mankind. And yet, despite the ignorance in which he keeps her, she has charms that can utterly bewitch, more seductive than the most cunning courtesan. But perhaps you've seen this angel of whom I speak.

ARNOLPHE
What is her name? Where does she live?

HORACE
Right here, in this fine mansion. And her name is Agnes.

ARNOLPHE
Staggers. Good God!

HORACE
Are you ill, sir?

ARNOLPHE
It's nothing. A sudden pain. It will pass.

HORACE
As it turns out, my darling girl—oh, if you could see her, Monsieur!

ARNOLPHE
Hell and damnation!

HORACE
But what is it?

ARNOLPHE
Another jab. Pay no attention.

HORACE
Do sit down then.

ARNOLPHE
    No matter. I'm fine. Please, tell me more.

HORACE
    It's really quite a story. The idiot who's locked her up
    is some man called La Zousse, or La Douche,
    something peculiar. God, what a fool he is!

ARNOLPHE
    A muttered cry. Arggh!

HORACE
    You really should sit, sir.

ARNOLPHE
    I think I will. Go on.

HORACE
    This idiot, whatever his name, is very rich but not
    very bright. All the town says he's an ass. Do you
    know him?

ARNOLPHE
    Aside. This is not to be believed!

HORACE
    I said, do you know him?

ARNOLPHE
    I may have heard of him.

HORACE
He's pathetic, is he not?

ARNOLPHE
Aside. The little wretch!

HORACE
Pardon?

ARNOLPHE
He is, in some ways, to be pitied, yes.

HORACE
And jealous too, no doubt. As if you could possess
such a jewel by locking it up.

ARNOLPHE
Indeed, it's not easy to keep one's treasure safe from
thieves.

HORACE
Oh sir, I adore her. What a sin for such a glorious
being to be left in the clutches of a greedy old fool.
But I'm determined to free her from his twisted grasp
and this purse, for which I am very grateful sir, will
help me achieve my goal. But you look disturbed.
Perhaps you don't approve?

ARNOLPHE
No, I was just thinking...

HORACE
I'm boring you, forgive me, but by God, she is heaven itself to me. I'll be back soon. But perhaps I shouldn't leave you alone?

ARNOLPHE
No, do. By all means.

HORACE
Again, sir, discretion, I beg you. Don't share my secret with anyone.

ARNOLPHE
Don't worry. I won't.

Exit, HORACE.

ARNOLPHE
I can't believe it.

HORACE returns.

HORACE
Above all, don't tell my father. He'll throw a fit.

ARNOLPHE
You can trust me as far as I can trust you.

HORACE
Thank you sir! What a fool that de la Douche is!

Exit, HORACE.

ARNOLPHE
  God, what suffering! It's not to be endured! How
  stupid he was to reveal it all to me—to me! He didn't
  know I'd taken a new title. Still, what a bumbler I
  am. I should have made him stay until I knew
  everything. How far has he gone? What did he say?
  That he had hopes. Hopes! I have to find out what's
  happened so far. If he's gotten to her it's the fault of
  those idiot servants!

ARNOLPHE knocks at the door.

Scene 5

_____

ARNOLPHE, ALAIN, GEORGETTE.

ALAIN
   I hope it's not me again.

ARNOLPHE
   Answer the door idiot!

GEORGETTE
   It's you all right.

ARNOLPHE
   Both of you come here. Hurry!

GEORGETTE
   Please sir, you're frightening me!

ALAIN
   Don't beat us, your honor!

ARNOLPHE
   So this is what you've been up to in my absence?
   You've betrayed me!

GEORGETTE
   He's going to eat us alive!

ALAIN
   He must have been bit by a rabid dog!

GEORGETTE
What did we do?

ALAIN
We never do anything!

ARNOLPHE
You scoundrels! While I was gone you let a man
into the house!

ALAIN and GEORGETTE try to escape.

GEORGETTE
Not me!

ALAIN
I don't know what you mean!

ARNOLPHE
Snatching them back. Now tell me, how did that man
get into my house? Quickly!

GEORGETTE
I forget!

ALAIN
I forget too!

ARNOLPHE
By God, I'll beat you until you remember!

GEORGETTE
  I'm dying!

ALAIN
  I'm already dead!

ARNOLPHE throws them aside.

ARNOLPHE
  Idiots! *To himself.* I wouldn't believe anything they'd
  tell me anyway. God, if I had known when I saw that
  boy years ago in his cradle what misery he'd bring
  me! I must have the truth. I'll get it from her. She's
  too innocent to lie. *To GEORGETTE and ALAIN.*
  Get up you two. Go inside and call Agnes. Wait.
  Aside. That's no good. They'll warn her that
  something's wrong. Best to go in myself. That way
  she'll suspect nothing. *To GEORGETTE and ALAIN.*
  Wait here.

Exit, ARNOLPHE.

Scene 6

ALAIN, GEORGETTE.

GEORGETTE
God help us, he's in a blind rage!

ALAIN
He's mad about that young man, just like I told you he would be.

GEORGETTE
But why does he order us to hide the mistress the way he does, and keep her locked up, and never get outside, and never let a man near her?

ALAIN
It's jealousy.

GEORGETTE
But how did he get like that?

ALAIN
It comes from being jealous.

GEORGETTE
Jealous over what?

ALAIN
Let me tell you how it is, Georgette. Jealousy is a thing, well, a thing that makes a man crazy on

account of he's so jealous. Let me just give you a little example. Suppose you were eating soup, and you saw me eyeballing your soup and waiting for a chance when you weren't looking to get that soup away from you and finish it all myself. What would you do?

GEORGETTE
I'd smack you with the ladle and go on eating.

ALAIN
Yes, but a man like our master isn't as reasonable as all that. By his way of looking at it, woman is the soup of man, and everyone is out to stick his spoon into someone else's dish.

GEORGETTE
Yes, but not everybody feels the same. Some husbands don't seem to mind *who* their wives sit down to table with, or who's dipping their spoons into what.

ALAIN
It's true, not every man's the greedy kind. Some are so busy feeding their faces at other men's tables they don't care what's on the menu at home.

GEORGETTE
He's coming back.

ALAIN
And he's not happy.

GEORGETTE
He never is.

Enter, ARNOLPHE.

Scene 7

ARNOLPHE, ALAIN, GEORGETTE.

ARNOLPHE
Aside. A Greek philosopher once advised the famous Alexander, should something put him in a rage, to say the alphabet first to give himself time to think before he acted. I've said it five times now, and I'm not sure it's enough yet. Still I must face the girl. I've asked her to join me for a little stroll around the square. I'll trick her into telling me everything and she'll never suspect what I'm up to. *Calling out.* Come, Agnes! Are you ready dear? *To ALAIN and GEORGETTE.* Go away you two. Get back inside and no more disobedience.

ALAIN
Don't worry about us, your honor.

Enter AGNES, exit ALAIN, GEORGETTE.

ARNOLPHE
Here she is. If only she'll lay my suspicions to rest.

Scene 8

ARNOLPHE, AGNES.

ARNOLPHE
Come, my dear. The weather's very fine, is it not?

AGNES
Oh, yes.

ARNOLPHE
Most pleasant.

AGNES
Indeed!

ARNOLPHE
What news, my child. Do you have any interesting little stories to tell me?

AGNES
I do, but...

ARNOLPHE
But?

AGNES
It's too terrible. You won't want to hear.

ARNOLPHE
Concerned. I won't? Still, it must be told.

AGNES
You'll be as heartbroken as I.

ARNOLPHE
I hope not. But tell, please. I must hear.

AGNES
Well, you see, it's about my dear little pussy.

ARNOLPHE
Pardon?

AGNES
It died. *She buries her face in her hands.* The precious little black and white one with the adorable mittens.

ARNOLPHE
Mastering himself. There, there my dear. All cats are mortal. I'm sure it's very sad, but we'll get you another little kitten, and all will be well, won't it?

AGNES
Do you promise?

ARNOLPHE
Of course. Now what else? While I was away was the weather bad? Did it rain?

AGNES
Oh no, the weather was wonderful. Every day more perfect than the last.

ARNOLPHE
No doubt with me gone, you were bored?

AGNES
Not at all.

ARNOLPHE
I see. Then what did you do during that whole long ten days that the time passed so quickly?

AGNES
Six nightshirts and six nightcaps.

ARNOLPHE
And that's all you did?

AGNES
Not all. I did more than that.

ARNOLPHE
More?

AGNES
I did a lace nightie for myself. Was that bad and selfish of me? Everything else was for you.

ARNOLPHE
Relief. My darling Agnes, what a vicious place the world is. What wicked gossip one hears.

AGNES
And what is gossip?

ARNOLPHE
It's when people talk.

AGNES
Oh, but I like that very much.

ARNOLPHE
But this is bad talk.

AGNES
And what makes it bad?

ARNOLPHE
Let me give you an example. Some people actually claim that while I was gone there was a certain strange young man who came to call and you received him. Of course I never believed for an instant such a foul slander.

AGNES
But why didn't you? You should have.

ARNOLPHE
What? Is it true then that you actually let a man enter the house?

AGNES
Oh, he did more than enter it. He was in and out of it constantly.

ARNOLPHE
Aside. God in heaven!

AGNES
You're not angry, are you?

ARNOLPHE
No, just surprised. *Aside.* The fact that she answers so readily must mean she's still untouched. *To AGNES.* I gave strict orders, Agnes, that no one was to be admitted. You were to see nobody at all, especially not a young man.

AGNES
It's true, I disobeyed you, but when I tell you how it happened you'll agree that you would have done exactly the same thing.

ARNOLPHE
We'll see about that. Tell me what happened.

AGNES
You see I was sitting on the balcony...

ARNOLPHE
Doing what?

AGNES
Sewing, when along came a young man.

ARNOLPHE
Where?

AGNES
In the street below. Oh, he was so handsome.

ARNOLPHE
And what did you do?

AGNES
I jumped up to see him better.

ARNOLPHE
Struggling to control himself. And then?

AGNES
And then, when he saw I had noticed him, he bowed.
I, not wanting to seem any less polite than he,
nodded at him and smiled.

ARNOLPHE
You did?

AGNES
You see how well I've been taught? And at once he
bowed to me again, and I nodded again, and he
bowed again, and I nodded again, and he bowed
again, and I nodded again...

ARNOLPHE
Yes, yes, everyone bowed. And then what?

AGNES
And then he went away.

ARNOLPHE
Thank God.

AGNES
But he came right back and started blowing kisses.

ARNOLPHE
What!

AGNES
Don't worry. I did the same. I returned every one.

ARNOLPHE
You've been very well taught indeed.

AGNES
I knew you'd be proud. What a fine figure he was, so tall and upright, and every time he raised himself after every bow, he seemed even more erect!

ARNOLPHE
Aside. No doubt. *To AGNES.* But surely that was the end of it?

AGNES
Yes.

ARNOLPHE
Thank heavens.

AGNES
Until the next day.

ARNOLPHE
What? More?

AGNES
Oh, so much more! You wouldn't believe what he
was capable of! I learned so much about how young
men are.

ARNOLPHE
How lucky. Keep going.

AGNES
The next day I never left the balcony, hoping he
would appear. But instead an old woman came by.
She seemed so distressed that I asked her what was
wrong, and she said, "May heaven bless you, dear
girl, and keep your beauty for many a year. But God
did not bestow such gifts on you to do harm, did
He?" "What do you mean," I asked. "Do you not
know the suffering you've caused someone who
never did you harm," she answered.

ARNOLPHE
The old witch! Damn her to Hell!

AGNES
"But what suffering have I caused," I asked? "The
victim," she said, "is that poor boy you gazed at
yesterday from your balcony." "But how could I
have injured him," I asked. "With what?" "It was
your eyes," she said. "They caused him so much pain
that even now he suffers." "Good heavens, Madam,"
I said. "Is there some evil power in my eyes that

makes boys sick?" And she said, "Yes, your eyes can pierce them to the heart and even make them die."

ARNOLPHE
Die! What rubbish.

AGNES
Oh no, she said it was so, and if he didn't get help right away he would fade away entirely. Imagine, that wonderful young man! And he had done nothing at all to me!

ARNOLPHE
Not yet, at least.

AGNES
And what if he had died? I can't bear to see anything suffer.

ARNOLPHE
Yes, yes. Go on.

AGNES
"But is there anything I can do," I asked? "There is," she said, "All he needs is to sit with you awhile. Your eyes, which caused all his suffering, hold the very cure that now can save him." How relieved I was. I said he should come as quickly as possible and I'd do everything I could to make him well. And he did. And I did.

ARNOLPHE
What did you do?

AGNES
Everything he wanted.

ARNOLPHE
Everything!

AGNES
How else could I have cured him?

ARNOLPHE
But what did he have you do?

AGNES
Oh, the most interesting things. You'd never guess.

ARNOLPHE
I might.

AGNES
You see how well I behaved?

ARNOLPHE
Aside. I've brought this on myself! And I still don't really know what happened!

AGNES
But what's wrong? You seem unhappy. Was there something bad in what I did?

ARNOLPHE
No, but go on. I want all the details. What else
happened?

AGNES
It was a miracle how quickly all his sickness
disappeared! And how happy he was and how
attentive and grateful! He gave me a lovely little
jewel case, and he gave coins to Alain and
Georgette, and they seemed so happy. You would
have loved him too!

ARNOLPHE
And when you were alone, what did you do?

AGNES
He said he loved me! Isn't that wonderful? And after
only seeing me once! And he said lots of other pretty
things and they were so sweet that I asked him to say
them over and over again. And then I began to feel
peculiar. My heart fluttered and I felt short of breath
and I felt very queer all over. A kind of tingling. I
never felt anything so nice.

ARNOLPHE
Aside. Oh strange torture, when the inquisitor is the
one who suffers most! *To AGNES.* But besides these
pretty words, did he try to kiss you?

AGNES
He didn't try.

ARNOLPHE
Thank God.

AGNES
He did.

ARNOLPHE
What misery!

AGNES
Not at all! It was wonderful. He showed me how! I told him I had never kissed anyone before, but he was so kind and said it didn't matter because he would teach me everything I needed to know.

ARNOLPHE
What a thoughtful, considerate young person!

AGNES
I knew you would approve!

ARNOLPHE
And what else? Did he caress you?

AGNES
Yes! And I caressed him too. At first, when he was still ill, he seemed so weak and limp that I was sure he was about to expire. But soon, with nothing more than a few embraces, he was quite recovered and ready for anything! How marvelous it was to behold the effect I had on him!

ARNOLPHE
Aside. God in heaven! *To AGNES.* And then?

AGNES
Suddenly shy. And then?

ARNOLPHE
Yes, and then? Was there more?

AGNES
More?

ARNOLPHE
To himself, in pain. Aghh! *To AGNES.* Yes, after the kissing!

AGNES
I can't.

ARNOLPHE
You must!

AGNES
But I'm afraid you'll be angry.

ARNOLPHE
No!

AGNES
Yes, you will.

ARNOLPHE
  I have to know the truth!

AGNES
  Promise you won't be angry?

ARNOLPHE
  Just tell me!

AGNES
  Well, I gave him, or at least, he took...

ARNOLPHE
  What?

AGNES
  I couldn't help it! I didn't know how to say no. I
  knew it wouldn't be fair to you, but I gave in at last.

ARNOLPHE
  To what? What did he take? What did you give him?

AGNES
  You'll be so disappointed. It's best if I don't tell.

ARNOLPHE
  No, no, no, no! Let's have the end of this mystery.
  What did he take from you?

AGNES
  He took...

ARNOLPHE
Aside. This is the suffering of the damned!

AGNES
He took...

ARNOLPHE
What?

AGNES
I gave him...

ARNOLPHE
What? What, damn you?

AGNES
...The pretty little handkerchief you gave me. He
said he'd treasure it always. And then he left.

ARNOLPHE
He did nothing more?

AGNES
Was there more to do? If only he had told me. I'd
have done anything!

ARNOLPHE
Takes a deep breath. God, what an escape! *To
AGNES.* Agnes, my dear, your innocence is your
greatest gift. I won't reproach you for what's too late
to undo. We'll forget all about it.

AGNES
Oh no, I won't do that.

ARNOLPHE
Believe me, all that worthless young man wants to
do is deceive you and then boast about it.

AGNES
Oh no, he said just the opposite, at least twenty
times.

ARNOLPHE
You don't know how clever these liars and cheats
are. Agnes, listen to me. To accept a jewel case and
his compliments about your pretty face and to go
along when he wants to kiss you and to let yourself
feel "queer" all over is a mortal sin, one of the
greatest you can commit.

AGNES
A mortal sin? But why?

ARNOLPHE
It just is. Everyone knows that.

AGNES
But the nuns said sin was ugly, and this was
beautiful.

ARNOLPHE
That's Satan trying to fool you. And if you go around
kissing men you will be damned to Hell.

AGNES
Then I'll never kiss anyone again. Not him. Not you.
Not anyone.

ARNOLPHE
Now, now. Let's not overdo it. What I meant to say
is... Well, look here, you're old enough to start
learning about these things. All these kisses and
caresses are fine, but only when they are done in the
right way.

AGNES
But I'm sure he did it in the right way.

ARNOLPHE
I mean, when you are married. Then there's no harm
in it.

AGNES
Then let me marry this instant!

ARNOLPHE
How happy I am to hear you say that. It's just what I
want too.

AGNES
You do?

ARNOLPHE
That's why I'm here.

AGNES
I never know when people are teasing me. Are you telling the truth?

ARNOLPHE
I swear it.

AGNES
We're to be married?

ARNOLPHE
Yes.

AGNES
But when?

ARNOLPHE
Tomorrow.

AGNES
Tomorrow? Oh, how happy you've made me.

She hugs him.

ARNOLPHE
I'm very glad you're so pleased.

AGNES
More than you know. I'm so grateful. He'll be so grateful too.

ARNOLPHE
  What's that?

AGNES
  He'll be grateful, too. Him.

ARNOLPHE
  Him?

AGNES
  My handsome young man. Who else?

ARNOLPHE
  Me, you blockhead! You're marrying me!

AGNES
  You?

ARNOLPHE
  Of course.

AGNES
  Oh, no. I couldn't do that.

ARNOLPHE
  And why not?

AGNES
  Because I love *him*.

ARNOLPHE
  Love him! You don't know what you're saying.

AGNES
I certainly do. He taught me all about it.

ARNOLPHE
You're going to be taught, all right. By me! You're going to learn obedience and duty! You've seen the last of that young wretch.

AGNES
No, I haven't. He's coming today.

ARNOLPHE
If he does, it's for the last time, and by God you'll send him away with a message he'll remember. When he arrives, you're to slam the door in his face!

AGNES
His handsome face?

ARNOLPHE
Yes!

AGNES
But he'd only stay outside and keep knocking.

ARNOLPHE
Then you'll hurl a flower pot at him. That should knock the lovesickness out of his head!

AGNES
I could never do that.

ARNOLPHE
You will, and I will make sure that you do!

AGNES
She starts to cry. But I don't have the heart to be so unkind...

ARNOLPHE
Then find it! I'm master of this house, and I've spoken. Go now and obey!

AGNES
But why do you...

ARNOLPHE
Stop your blubbering, damn you! Your tears mean nothing to me!

AGNES
But I'm so miserable...

ARNOLPHE
No, you're not. I forbid it. You'll be happy or else.

Exit, AGNES, followed by ARNOLPHE.

Scene 9

AGNES, HORACE, ARNOLPHE.

AGNES at a window. HORACE appears below. AGNES is charmed. She notices ARNOLPHE watching from the side. She throws a flower pot at him.

Exit, HORACE. Exit, AGNES above.

Scene 10

ARNOLPHE, AGNES, ALAIN, GEORGETTE.

ARNOLPHE
You've done well, Agnes, and so have you two. By following my instructions so completely you've put that young devil to flight. That's what they are, Agnes, sons of Satan. They may dress well, and have handsome faces under their foppish hats, and a fine shape under their fashionable clothes, but what do those things conceal? The scales of a serpent, and the cloven hoof! And just think, one of them had you in his hands! But thanks to my watchful care, you escaped. And the way you hurled that flower pot at him! How surprised he was, how he cringed! And then he stooped to pick it up as if he couldn't believe his eyes! I laughed so hard I had to turn away. But now, I want a word with you alone, Agnes. Off you go, you two. I hope you've finally learned how to protect your master's property.

GEORGETTE
Don't worry sir, that young man doesn't stand a chance with us.

ALAIN
You can say that again. Those coins he gave us? They were fakes.

ARNOLPHE
Well, here's some real money. Now go buy food for
the dinner I am giving for my friend, Chrysalde, and
then one of you, on your way back, fetch the notary.
Tell him there's an important contract to prepare.

Exit, ALAIN, GEORGETTE.

Scene 11

ARNOLPHE, AGNES.

ARNOLPHE
Agnes, put down your sewing and listen to what I
have to say. Look at me directly and don't turn away.
My dear, I am going to marry you. Do you know
how lucky you are?

AGNES
No.

ARNOLPHE
Then let me tell you. What were you when I found
you?

AGNES
Very little.

ARNOLPHE
Yes, but *what* were you?

AGNES
A girl.

ARNOLPHE
You were nothing, that's what you were. Living in
poverty. No future but hard work and drudgery. And
what will you be tomorrow?

AGNES
  Myself?

ARNOLPHE
  Yes, but more importantly, you will be my wife, the
  wife of a rich man, a respected man, living a life of
  leisure and privilege And I bestow this honor on *you*,
  when I could have taken a wife a dozen times in the
  past. I'm giving you a name, do you understand?
  Bear it with such propriety that I shall never have
  cause to regret my choice. Marriage, Agnes, is not to
  be taken lightly and of the wife requires an austerity
  of soul. Will you remember that?

AGNES
  I'm certain you will remind me.

ARNOLPHE
  I do not so exalt you in order for you to lead a
  frivolous life. Remember, yours is the weaker sex. It
  is in the male that all power rightfully resides. And
  though there are two halves to mankind, those two
  are not equal. One commands, the other obeys. One
  leads, the other follows. And that's not just in
  marriage, it is in everything in life.

AGNES
  Is it?

ARNOLPHE
It is. The devotion a soldier shows his general, or a servant his master, or a child its father, is nothing compared to the submission a wife must show the man who is her master. If he fixes a stern look upon her, she should lower her eyes and dare not look upon him again until that look is one of tenderness. Don't imitate those flirts whose loose behavior is the talk of all the gossips in town, or who allow idle young men to dally with them. Remember that in marrying you I put my good name in your safekeeping. Honor is a pure thing and cannot survive the slightest stain. Betray my honor and what waits for you in Hell is a cauldron of boiling pitch that will turn you black.

AGNES
How awful!

ARNOLPHE
But you need have no fear of that as long as you obey me in everything. Here, show me how well you read.

He hands her a book.

AGNES
What is it?

ARNOLPHE
It is a kind of holy book written by a very wise man.

AGNES
Anonymous? What a strange name.

ARNOLPHE
Pay no attention. He seeks no glory for himself. He
only wishes to teach all the wives of the world the
right way to behave. I want you to learn it by heart.
Then, when we're married, you'll recite these
maxims to me when you say your prayers.

AGNES
Reading. "The Secrets of Marriage." Oh I like the
title!

ARNOLPHE
Remember, you can have no secrets from me.

AGNES
None?

ARNOLPHE
None at all. Now read.

AGNES
Reading. "The Secrets of Marriage; or the Maxims
of a Dutiful Wife. First maxim: she who shares her
bed in wedlock must remember to let no other into it
than the man who brought her there."

ARNOLPHE
No doubt you find that confusing.

AGNES

I do. Why would I want to sleep three in a bed?

ARNOLPHE

I'll explain later. Continue.

AGNES

"Second maxim. Of fancy clothes she has no need other than what pleases her husband. Better for her to remain naked and hide at home than prance about in public looking to draw attention to herself." Must I be naked then?

ARNOLPHE

No, but you'll dress only to please me. Go on.

AGNES

"Third maxim. She shall not paint her face. Creams and rouges are meant to please only her vanity and attract her lovers." Do women paint their faces then?

ARNOLPHE

Only the very bad ones.

AGNES

And does it attract their lovers?

ARNOLPHE

I'm afraid so.

AGNES

So I mayn't try?

ARNOLPHE
No, you may not. Continue.

AGNES
"Fourth maxim. She shall accept no presents from
other men. Nothing is given for free, and what she is
meant to give back belongs only to her husband."

ARNOLPHE
And you've already violated that one.

AGNES
But I gave nothing in return.

ARNOLPHE
You almost gave what you could never get back.
Read on.

AGNES
"Fifth maxim. When gentlemen come to call..." Oh
good!

ARNOLPHE
Not necessarily. As you'll see.

AGNES
"When gentlemen come to call, she should turn them
away. No man belongs in her husband's house but
his friends alone, and even they only when he is
present." How dull marriage sounds.

ARNOLPHE
Virtue is not meant to be exciting. It is meant to be rewarding.

AGNES
But where is the reward for the wife?

ARNOLPHE
In Heaven. Keep going.

AGNES
"Sixth maxim. A wife should give no balls or parties nor attend those to which she is invited. They are nothing but the flesh markets at which young gallants first survey the wares and then make off with the goods." But why should they do that?

ARNOLPHE
Why indeed? But enough. Read the rest of them to yourself. I'll come back later and explain anything you don't understand. I have some business I must settle. Go in and treat this precious volume with the devotion it deserves. If the notary comes, tell him to have a seat and wait.

Exit, AGNES.

Scene 12

ARNOLPHE.

ARNOLPHE
What could be safer than to marry her? She's like a lump of wax and I can shape her any way I like. True, she was almost snatched away from me while I was gone, but that was only due to her simplicity. If a wife is to have a fault, that is the best direction in which to err. A simple wife is easy to correct. A little talk and she is set right. A clever one is something else entirely. Whatever she wants she'll have at any cost and no amount of reasoning will dissuade her. She's able to make her vices sound like virtues, her crimes like acts of honor, her betrayals like loyalty itself. She twists and turns every word to her own devices, mocks at principle, and contrives her intrigues with such ingenuity that the shrewdest man is deceived. Against her schemes and strategies there is no defense. Once she's determined to give away her husband's honor, there's nothing for him to do but accept his fate. But this young devil won't have the chance to gloat over my disgrace. He talks too much—the fault of all Frenchmen. But here he comes. I must conceal my feelings and see if I can get his sad little tale out of him. What consolation it will bring me.

Enter, HORACE.

Scene 13

_____

ARNOLPHE, HORACE.

HORACE
> There you are! I've been to your house again and again today but I always found you out. I'm so pleased that now I have the joy...

ARNOLPHE
> Come, no fine talk. I'd be just as happy to see this vile custom stamped out. Men waste half the day in empty words. Let's simply say what we have to say. Tell me, how's your love affair progressing? I was a little distracted the last time we met, but now I can't wait to hear all the details.

HORACE
> Alas, since I opened my heart to you I feared all my hopes were dashed.

ARNOLPHE
> How dreadful! What happened?

HORACE
> My beloved's wretched guardian has returned from the country.

ARNOLPHE
> Bad news.

HORACE

What's more, he seems to have found out about all
our meetings when he was away.

ARNOLPHE

But I thought they were in secret? How did he find
out, and so quickly?

HORACE

I don't know, but I'm convinced he has. I went to my
love's window at the usual hour to pay homage to
her beauty and found the servants entirely against
me. Instead of welcoming me as usual, they threw
me out and slammed the door in my face!

ARNOLPHE

In your face?

HORACE

Can you believe it?

ARNOLPHE

Shocking. Tell me more.

HORACE

I asked them what was wrong and begged them to let
me come inside, but whatever I said they
answered—"Go away! The master says you're never
to come inside again!"

ARNOLPHE

Never?

HORACE
Never! What a bleak sentence! And then, to top it off, while I was still trying to catch her eye, she opened the window and—no doubt on orders from her miserable captor—threw a flower pot at my head!

ARNOLPHE
At your head? Did she hit you?

HORACE
Very nearly. Luckily, I ducked. Not exactly the love token I was hoping for.

ARNOLPHE
Damn it, my boy, that does look pretty bad.

HORACE
Yes, I'm afraid the old fool's return spoiled everything.

ARNOLPHE
You have my deepest sympathy.

HORACE
He wrecked my plan entirely.

ARNOLPHE
I'm sure it's not as bad as all that. You'll find a way to fight back.

HORACE
  With a little help, I believe I shall.

ARNOLPHE
  That should be easy. You say the lady loves you,
  doesn't she?

HORACE
  I'm certain of it.

ARNOLPHE
  Then you'll figure out something.

HORACE
  I certainly will.

ARNOLPHE
  You shouldn't be scared off by a flower pot.

HORACE
  I won't. I could tell at once the old idiot was behind
  everything. But what amazed me was something *she*
  did, which you'd never expect of a girl of such
  innocence.

ARNOLPHE
  Concerned. Really?

HORACE
  Yes! Love is indeed a wondrous teacher, sir! It can
  make us into what we never were—the miser into a

spendthrift, the coward into a lion, the shy man full
of fire...

ARNOLPHE
Yes, but what did she do?

HORACE
Love spurs us on and can turn even the most naive
maiden into the most ingenious deceiver...

ARNOLPHE
Fine, yes, very well, but what? What?

HORACE
Wait till you hear. Before she threw the flower pot,
she looked at me and shouted, very loudly, "Go
away young man. I've heard everything you have to
say, and thought about it, and *here* is my answer!"
And then she threw the flower pot. But guess what
was inside the flower pot?

ARNOLPHE
What?

HORACE
A letter! Doesn't that show the greatest cunning?

ARNOLPHE
It does.

HORACE
Laughing. And as for her idiot guardian, doesn't she

make him look an ass?

ARNOLPHE
More than you think.

HORACE
But you look unwell again. Would you like to sit?

ARNOLPHE
I'm fine. Just a little relapse.

HORACE
God, what a fool.

ARNOLPHE
So he is.

HORACE
Yet you're not quite as amused as I thought you
would be.

ARNOLPHE
It will come to me.

HORACE
But let me show you the letter she wrote. You can
tell me whether I'm right in thinking she's bound to
be mine, and there's nothing her oppressor can do
about it.

ARNOLPHE
We shall see.

HORACE
Oh no, I assure you. I can more than outwit him.
Would you like to hear what she has to say?

ARNOLPHE
I can't wait.

HORACE
What an angel! She puts everything in the most
touching way. Her artless manner, the purity of her
mind, nature itself could not better express true
love's awakening, or so I think.

ARNOLPHE
Just read the damned thing!

HORACE
I knew you'd be interested. *Reading.* "I must write to
you but I don't know what words to use. I know now
that I have been brought up to know nothing at all
about anything so I'm afraid to say the wrong way all
the things that are in my heart. Truly, I don't know
what you've done to me but I know that I am very
sad to have to do the mean things I am made to do to
you and that it would be the most painful thing in the
world to give you up and I don't want to and would
be much happier if I was yours instead. This is a
good example of the kind of thing that might be the
wrong thing to say but in any case I can't help saying
it and wish I could have you without there being
anything wrong in that though I'm told there is. They

all say, my guardian, the servants and everyone, that all young men are deceivers and that I shouldn't believe anything they say and that whatever you've said to me is just a trick. But I can't believe that of you. Your words touch me so deeply that I think they must be true. Please say very honestly what you intend, and if you are planning to deceive me please tell me so directly because my own intentions are blameless, and if yours are not I think it would be very mean and wicked of you to do that to me and I would die of despair."

ARNOLPHE
The little bitch!

HORACE
Pardon?

ARNOLPHE
Nothing. I said I have an itch.

ARNOLPHE
Was ever anything so dear? Despite the tyranny she lives under, she remains sweet beyond compare. It's the basest crime on earth to stifle such a spirit. Our love has awakened her, and if it's the last thing I do, I'll free her from that heartless beast, that villain, that brute, that ogre, that...

ARNOLPHE
I think you should go now.

HORACE
But why? There's so much more I must...

ARNOLPHE
Not now. I have an urgent appointment. I'll see you later.

HORACE
But I must have your help. I'm barred from the house. The servants are against me. I had an old woman who was an expert in these affairs, but they've driven her away too. Don't you know anyone who could help?

ARNOLPHE
Sorry. You'll figure it out. Now leave me be.

HORACE
Farewell, then, if I must. Please sir, be discreet!

Exit, HORACE.

Scene 14

ARNOLPHE.

ARNOLPHE
Every time I'm with that boy I suffer the torment of
the damned! To think the girl could prove so sly.
The little vixen, sitting there, smiling at me so
obediently and all the while planning her deceit!
Betrayer! Either she's fooled me from the start and
never was what she seemed, or Hell's got a hold of
her and is teaching a student with natural gifts! That
damned letter! It's clear that young ass has turned
her head and made her forget all about the love and
devotion she owes to me. This loss is a double
torment, my honor stolen and her love as well! Him
in my place. All those years of planning wasted!
Fine! Let him have her! We all know where that
would end. He'd tire of her soon enough. Then let
her come begging back to me and see what I'd do.

But I can't. I can't. All the years I cared for her, and
watched her grow, picturing the future, seeing her
become more and more perfect before my eyes! And
then to allow another to pluck the ripe fruit from the
tree? All wasted because of a girlish crush! She has
nothing without me! I could put her in the street this
instant!

And yet, what do I feel in spite of all this? That I love her unbearably and cannot give her up! Fool! Idiot! Have you no shame? Aren't you willing to punish her for her crimes? I'll go inside for a little while. I'll see if she remains determined to conceal her treachery from me. Perhaps she'll have a change of heart. Heaven, look down and show me pity. Let no dishonor stain my brow, or if fate will have it that I must suffer this indignity, let me suffer it in secret with none knowing it but me.

END ACT I

ACT II

Scene 1

ARNOLPHE.

Entering from within.

ARNOLPHE

I can't keep still. Every moment I'm devising some new strategy to prevent that vermin from satisfying his lust. How calm the little traitor was when I went in just now. Despite her load of sin, she acts like a saint. The more she sat, so calm and cool, the more furious I became. Yet, strange to say, the more enraged at her I become, the more I want her. Desperate as I am, longing to punish her, her beauty has never seemed so great. Never did her bright eyes so strike me or her spirit so captivate me. Cruel joke of fate! Have I spent years of loving care on her protection, sheltered her since she was a tiny creature, cherished dreams of our future together, and based all my hopes of happiness on her for this? Some dandy prances onto the scene at the last moment and snatches the prize from my very fingers, and just when I was all but wed? No, my young friend. I swear you will not. However sly your schemes, you won't have the last laugh on me.

Enter, NOTARY.

Scene 2

ARNOLPHE, NOTARY.

NOTARY
> Good day, sir. I am the notary you sent for. So, you
> have a contract you wish to draw up?

ARNOLPHE
> *Unaware that the NOTARY has arrived.* But how?
> How shall it be done?

NOTARY
> Well, according to the law, naturally.

ARNOLPHE
> *Still unaware.* Yes, but I must be prudent. I have to
> proceed carefully.

NOTARY
> Of course, sir. You can rely on me to act only in
> your interests.

ARNOLPHE
> *Same.* One must always prepare for the unexpected.

NOTARY
> Quite true, sir. But in my hands you can be assured
> that you'll be thoroughly protected. For example,
> don't execute the contract until the dowry's been paid
> in full.

ARNOLPHE

Same. I must act in secret. If this gets out, all the gossips in town will have a field day.

NOTARY

If that's your concern I suppose it's possible we could draw up the contract in secret. It's not usual, mind, and I won't be party to anything illegal. On the other hand...

ARNOLPHE

Same. But how shall I deal with her? What does she deserve?

NOTARY

Well, in the ordinary way of going about things, the bride's share of the dowry is proportional.

ARNOLPHE

Same. Still, it's hard to be brutal to a girl you adore.

NOTARY

If that's your wish, you could always increase what you allow her. Within reason, of course.

ARNOLPHE

Same. I cannot decide which way to go.

NOTARY

If it's any help, sir, the husband ordinarily gives the bride an entitlement equal to one-third of the total

dowry, but that's a matter of custom, not law, so if
you choose to increase that sum...

ARNOLPHE
Same. I must...

He turns and sees the NOTARY for the first time.

NOTARY
As for the division of property in case of death, the
husband can provide as he feels suitable.

ARNOLPHE
What the devil?

NOTARY
It's not that shocking. The wife has no rights in the
matter, of course. It's strictly the husband's decision
to make. He can make certain of his wife's security
by jointure, or settlement whereby if the lady
predeceases her husband the gift is canceled, or it
can revert to her heirs, if so agreed, or go by
common law, or a deed of gift appended to the
original instrument.

ARNOLPHE
What *is* all this?

NOTARY
What it is what, sir? Why do you stare, sir? Do you
imply I do not know contracts? Do you imply I do
not know that spouses jointly hold, in vive, goods,

chattels, lands, and money unless one party renounces? Do you imply I do not know that one third of the bride's resources enters the joint estate...

ARNOLPHE
I imply nothing at all because I don't give a tinker's damn. Who asked for all this pedantic nonsense?

NOTARY
You did, sir! And now you have the nerve to treat me in this fashion, treating my expertise with ridicule?

ARNOLPHE
Stop talking rot. Be on your way, sir.

NOTARY
But you are the one who sent for me.

ARNOLPHE
I most certainly did not. But if I have need of a blithering idiot who can't mind his own business I'll certainly know who to send for. Now be off with you.

NOTARY
The man should be locked up.

Enter ALAIN, GEORGETTE.

Scene 3

ARNOLPHE, NOTARY, ALAIN, GEORGETTE.

NOTARY
> *To ALAIN, GEORGETTE.* Ah, here you are. Did your master send for me or did he not?

ALAIN
> He did.

NOTARY
> Then you can tell him from me that he's a horse's ass.

GEORGETTE
> We'll be sure to tell him, sir.

Exit, NOTARY.

Scene 4

ARNOLPHE, ALAIN, GEORGETTE.

ALAIN
Sir...

ARNOLPHE
Ah, come here, friends, my good and faithful servants.

GEORGETTE
The notary said to tell you...

ARNOLPHE
Yes, yes, we'll have time for that later. My honor is under attack and I know I can rely on you to help me to defend it. Think how shamed you would be if you had to go around town knowing your master's name had been dirtied. Imagine the sneers and jokes behind your back. You don't want that, do you? So since we're in this together, I need to know that I can depend on you to keep that young man from the house.

GEORGETTE
Don't worry, sir. We learned our lesson. You beat it into us.

ARNOLPHE
Beware his fancy words and flattery.

ALAIN
Just let him try to flatter us, sir!

GEORGETTE
Just let him try to find something to praise *us* about!

ARNOLPHE
What if he said, "Dear Alain, for pity's sake, do me a kindness." What would you say?

ALAIN
I'd say, "Get lost."

ARNOLPHE
Good, good. *To GEORGETTE.* And if he said "Georgette, I know your heart must be as kind as your face is pretty."

GEORGETTE
I'd say, "Leave my face out of it, fathead."

ARNOLPHE
Excellent. *To ALAIN.* "Come, Alain, let me in. You know my intentions are as pure as the driven snow."

ALAIN
As pure as you're purely a jackass!

ARNOLPHE
Very well said. *To GEORGETTE.* "Have pity on me, sweet Georgette, or my heart will break!"

GEORGETTE
Go break your neck, you big dumb oaf!

ARNOLPHE
Well done, Georgette. You've got the spirit of it now. But again, "Alain, Georgette, I'm not one to forget a favor. Here, take these coins. It's but a taste of how generous I can be to my true friends. All I ask is an hour or two in your young mistress's company."

Both take the money, then start shoving him back and forth.

GEORGETTE
Take that, deceiver!

ALAIN
And that, liar!

ARNOLPHE
Good...

GEORGETTE
And that, you bastard!

ALAIN
And that, you moron!

ARNOLPHE
Yes, good, but..

GEORGETTE
And that, fart face!

ALAIN
And that, douchebag!

ARNOLPHE
Good, good, but enough now.

ALAIN
And that, you miserable ass wipe!

GEORGETTE
And that, you lousy shit head!

ARNOLPHE
Enough!

They stop.

GEORGETTE
Was that right?

ALAIN
Did we do good?

ARNOLPHE
Yes, yes, very good except for the money. You
shouldn't have taken the money.

GEORGETTE
    We didn't think about that, sir.

ALAIN
    We got too caught up in our parts.

GEORGETTE
    Would you like to try it again?

ARNOLPHE
    No need, no need. Go back inside.

ALAIN
    Really sir, it's no trouble.

ARNOLPHE
    That will do! Go inside. You can keep the money.
    Just remember what you're supposed to do and be
    ready to support me.

Exit, ALAIN, GEORGETTE.

Scene 5

ARNOLPHE.

ARNOLPHE
The cobbler at the corner is a sharp-eyed man. I'll
enlist his aid as well. As for Agnes, I'll keep her
under lock and key, and anyone who approaches the
house to try to see her will be barred. No old
women, no hatmakers, no peddlers, no delivery
boys. I know all the little stratagems that lovers use
to advance their secret love affairs. That boy will
have to invent something new if he's to get any
message to her.

Enter, HORACE.

Scene 6

ARNOLPHE, HORACE.

HORACE
What luck to find you here again! I've just had a narrow escape.

ARNOLPHE
Indeed?

HORACE
Yes, I was lucky to get away.

ARNOLPHE
What happened, dear boy?

HORACE
Just after I left you, who did I chance to see on her balcony but the lovely Agnes! She had opened the window a moment before and happened to see me. She made a sign for me to wait, and somehow managed to steal downstairs to the garden and let me in. We went upstairs to her bedroom, and no sooner were we there then we heard her jealous guardian stamping up the stairs.

ARNOLPHE
What did you do?

HORACE
The ingenious Agnes! She pushed me into her wardrobe and just managed to close it when he burst in. I couldn't see anything, but I heard him marching back and forth, grumbling and barking to himself, knocking things over, kicking the dog. He finally broke a vase! Clearly the old goat was worked up about something. Probably he had suspicions that his captive was deceiving him in some way but was too stupid to figure it out. Finally, he left the room, slamming the door and pounding back down the stairs. Naturally, we didn't dare extend our rendezvous, since we knew he might come back at any moment.

ARNOLPHE
He might have indeed.

HORACE
But rest assured, I'll see her again tonight. We've arranged to meet after midnight. Here's our plan. I'll stand outside her window and cough three times.

ARNOLPHE
How clever.

HORACE
She'll open it wide and I, with a ladder I'll conceal ahead of time, will climb through her window and into our bower of bliss. The whole night shall be ours!

ARNOLPHE
You've got him fooled this time, don't you?

HORACE
Oh, we do. I tell you this because you're my only
friend. Somehow it's not possible to keep such joy to
oneself. But you share, I know, my happy
expectations, and are as excited for me as I am
myself.

ARNOLPHE
I can barely contain myself.

HORACE
But forgive me, farewell. I must get ready for
tonight!

Exit, HORACE.

Scene 7

ARNOLPHE.

ARNOLPHE
God, they'll hound me to death! Everything I devise
these two undo with their childish complicity! Shall
I, at the height of maturity, be made fool of by a
green girl and a hare-brained boy? For twenty years
I've carefully observed the follies of every man who
married unwisely. I've noted each slip and misstep,
and prided myself on how, when I finally took a
bride, I'd ward off every threat. Yet, for all that, here
I am, as if fate has determined that no man should
escape, as much a victim as any man I've mocked.

But no, it won't be! This girl is still mine. I won't let
her go! And though her heart has been stolen by this
little pest, that's as much of her as he'll get. This
evening's touching tryst won't go as smoothly as he'd
like. That's one thing I have on my rival—he's been
fool enough to make me his closest confidant!

Enter, CHRSYALDE.

Scene 8

ARNOLPHE, CHRYSALDE.

CHRYSALDE
Greetings, friend. Here I am, as you see, right on time. Shall we go in to dinner?

ARNOLPHE
The dinner's off.

CHRYSALDE
That's a little sudden.

ARNOLPHE
Forgive me. I have a crisis on my hands.

CHRYSALDE
Don't tell me your wedding plans have changed?

ARNOLPHE
None of your damned business.

CHRYSALDE
Come, come, don't be angry. Allow me to help. I judge by your angry face that I've touched on the source of this crisis.

ARNOLPHE
I don't need your help. And believe me, the last thing that is going to happen is some young gallant making a fool out of me.

CHRYSALDE
Odd that intelligent as you are, you remain obsessed with this idea. It's as if your only measure of happiness is whether or not you are deceived by your wife. Greed, envy, vice, cowardice, none of these seem to trouble you in the least. The only thing you find dishonorable is to be cuckolded. Now come, should a man consider himself robbed of his good name through some misfortune of which he is not the cause? Is our only way of judging a man is whether his wife goes astray? To a man of sense, there is nothing so crushing in these accidents of fate. I'm not condoning it, mind, not like some men that openly permit such scandal, or jest about it. But is it right to consider it the greatest crime of all, and foam and rage, and vow bloody vengeance? Between these two extremes there is a middle course. Cuckoldry need not be feared as some dire monster. You can live with it if you can take things calmly and make the best of an unpleasant thing.

ARNOLPHE
For that fine speech the esteemed fraternity of cuckolds owes you many thanks. I'm sure everyone, if they just heard your wisdom, would rush to join the brotherhood.

CHRYSALDE
I wouldn't want that either. Yet it's fate whether or not we choose wisely in our wives. It's best to take it like a wager in piquet. If you make a losing bet you accept it calmly and do the best you can with what remains in your hand.

ARNOLPHE
In other words, just turn a blind eye and keep telling yourself it's all right.

CHRYSALDE
Laugh if you want, my friend, but I can name fifty things that would cause me more distress than this misfortune you so fear. If I had to choose my poison, I'd rather be a cuckold than to be married to a woman of so-called high moral virtue, one of those shrews who never stops lecturing and judging, as violently chaste as an Amazon who, in payment for being faithful to us, insists on nagging us to death. I think, friend, you might find that cuckoldry is what you make of it, and might even have its compensations.

ARNOLPHE
I hope you get your wish, but before I'd allow such a thing, I swear...

CHRYSALDE
Don't swear or you may soon find yourself forsworn. If destiny will have it, all your oaths mean nothing.

ARNOLPHE
Me, a cuckold? Never.

CHRYSALDE
Don't let it fret you so. It happens to the best of men.

ARNOLPHE
Not to me. Enough of you now, you try my patience.

CHRYSALDE
So now you're annoyed with me? Well, well. Goodbye then. But bear in mind that, with all your proclamations that you'll never be cuckolded you're tempting fate to make you so.

Exit, CHRYSALDE.

ARNOLPHE
It won't happen. I shall not let it. In fact, I'll remove this threat at once. *Calls out.* Alain! Georgette!

Enter, ALAIN, GEORGETTE.

Scene 9

ARNOLPHE, ALAIN, GEORGETTE.

ALAIN
   Yes, sir?

GEORGETTE
   Do you want us to throw you out again, sir?

ARNOLPHE
   Loyal servants, the battle is joined and we must win.
   Your love for me, which you've proved so well, is
   called on now for this emergency. And if you act the
   way I expect, your reward shall be handsome.

ALAIN
   You can count on us sir.

GEORGETTE
   Especially if there's a handsome reward.

ARNOLPHE
   This very night—don't breathe a word to anyone—a
   certain rascal whom I think you know intends to
   scale the wall to get to Agnes. But we shall lay a
   little trap for him. You'll both be upstairs at the
   window, armed with clubs. And when the villain
   reaches the top rung of the ladder, I'll throw open the
   window, and you beat the living hell out of the

wretch. I want him so black and blue that he'll never even think of coming back. And, remember, don't call my name while you're beating him. I'll be hiding behind. Are you ready to serve me in this?

ALAIN
If blows are called for, I'm your man.

GEORGETTE
Don't worry, sir. I've been beaten all my life. I know just how to do it.

ARNOLPHE
Go in then and whatever you do, keep quiet.

They go back in.

ARNOLPHE
Tonight I'll teach the abused husbands of the world a little lesson in how to receive their wives' suitors. If they all got such a welcome as I have in mind, there would be a lot fewer cuckolds in the world.

Exit, ARNOLPHE.

Scene 10

ARNOLPHE, ALAIN, GEORGETTE.

Night. Noises off. After a moment, enter ARNOLPHE, cloaked, followed by ALAIN and GEORGETTE.

ARNOLPHE
   You idiots! I didn't say kill him!

ALAIN
   You wanted him black and blue!

ARNOLPHE
   Yes, not bloody and dead! And it's you two thick-witted cretins who are to blame! Did you see him in that heap at the foot of ladder? My God, what's to be done? It's a ghastly situation.

GEORGETTE
   Maybe we should go collect the body.

ARNOLPHE
   You'll only make matters worse. Don't disturb a thing until I figure out what to do. Go back in and keep silent as the grave.

Exit ALAIN, GEORGETTE.

ARNOLPHE
What a terrible situation. It's nearly daybreak. The
body will be found. I could say that the servants
thought he was a thief breaking into the house. That
much is true enough. But what will the boy's father
say, with him killed almost on my own doorstep?

Enter, HORACE.

Scene 11

ARNOLPHE, HORACE.

HORACE
Who's that? I'd better be careful.

ARNOLPHE
How could I have guessed... Wait. Who's there?
Speak up!

HORACE
Monsieur Arnolphe?

ARNOLPHE
Yes?

HORACE
Thank God, it's you. It's Horace again. I was
desperate to find you.

ARNOLPHE
To himself. God, no! I don't know whether to be
overjoyed or furious. *To HORACE.* Is that really
you, boy?

HORACE
Indeed it is, and I'm afraid I need your help again.
How wonderful you should appear so magically
every time I need you!

ARNOLPHE
Isn't it just? I can hardly believe it myself.

HORACE
My plans, I'm happy to report, have succeeded
beyond all expectations.

ARNOLPHE
What?

HORACE
You sound surprised.

ARNOLPHE
Not at all. I just didn't expect you to succeed so
soon.

HORACE
Yes, great success—in spite of an unfortunate
incident that might have upset them entirely. I don't
know how it happened, but somehow someone
learned of my midnight rendezvous with Agnes.

ARNOLPHE
You don't say?

HORACE
Incredible, but it happened. It was like they were
waiting for me.

ARNOLPHE
Imagine that. And did they catch you?

HORACE
Nearly. I was just at the top step of the ladder, about
to fold Agnes in my arms, when suddenly two
shadowy beasts jumped out of the dark and started
flailing away at me with bats or clubs or something.

ARNOLPHE
And did they beat you unmercifully?

HORACE
Thank God, no. They didn't seem too bright. They
just waved at the air and shouted a lot. But appearing
as suddenly as they did startled me, and I lost my
footing and tumbled down the ladder.

ARNOLPHE
You didn't die apparently.

HORACE
Luckily I fell on a bush.

ARNOLPHE
That is luck. And then?

HORACE
I just lay there motionless, hoping to trick them into
thinking I was dead.

ARNOLPHE
I suppose it worked.

HORACE
Like a charm. They all started screaming and cursing at each other, as frightened as could be. I was pretty certain I could hear the voice of that nincompoop who keeps her prisoner. He seemed the most frightened of all.

ARNOLPHE
How thrilled you must have been to outwit your rival.

HORACE
Oh, believe me, it takes nothing at all to outwit him. He's the dullest clod that lives. In any case, I heard them slam the window shut, and then I sneaked away. Just as I got to the garden wall, Agnes came hurrying out, worried sick, the darling lamb. While they were busy abusing each other, she had managed to slip out to find me. Imagine her joy when she found me completely unharmed.

ARNOLPHE
I can just imagine it.

HORACE
To be brief, guided by her own heart, the adorable girl has decided to flee the tyranny of her guardian and entrust her safety to me. Can you imagine what a brute he is in order to drive such a modest girl to such dire lengths? Think of the risk she'd run if I couldn't be trusted? But my love's too pure. She can

rely on me. I'd rather die than see the slightest harm
ever come to her. All I ask is to never leave her side.

ARNOLPHE
How blessed you are.

HORACE
Unfortunately my father won't see it like that. He'll
be angry at first, I know. But once he meets her he'll
understand everything. She'll win him over
completely, even if she hasn't a *sou*. And if he won't
budge, by God, I'd rather be disinherited than leave
her.

ARNOLPHE
You seem to have achieved everything you wanted.
What could you possibly need from me?

HORACE
It's a big favor, I know, but what I ask is this. Could
you possibly hide her away in your house for the
next few days? I ask this because I am determined to
throw her guardian off the scent. I can just picture
him now, as plain as if he was standing in front me.
He's so enraged that I don't know what he'd do.

ARNOLPHE
Really? It's just possible he might be feeling slightly
better just now.

HORACE
You don't know the monster.

ARNOLPHE
    True.

HORACE
    Besides, if she was even so much as seen with me
    for a moment, there would be talk of impropriety,
    and I would never permit her honor to be questioned.
    Dear friend, time and again you've allowed me to
    open my heart to you and you've refused me nothing.

ARNOLPHE
    Aside. Not that I haven't tried.

HORACE
    And now I ask this last, heroic service of you, to
    guard my treasure and my bride to be.

ARNOLPHE
    You can rely on me.

HORACE
    You'll grant me this favor?

ARNOLPHE
    Without hesitation. In fact, I can't tell you how
    happy it makes me to be there in your hour of need.
    Thank heaven you thought to ask me.

HORACE
    How kind you are! I feared you might refuse my
    rash request, but you're a man of the world, after all,
    who looks on young love with a kindly eye.

ARNOLPHE
None watches it more closely. Where is she?

HORACE
Just at the corner. My man is guarding her.

ARNOLPHE
It's almost daylight. Where should we meet?
Someone might see if you brought her straight to
me. And if you took her directly to my house it
would start the servants talking. We should look for
some shadowy place. How about this garden? I'll
wait there in the dark and then take her back myself,
concealed in a cloak.

HORACE
You're right, sir, we must be very careful. He might
be in the streets right now, searching for her. I'll go,
and bring her quickly to you there, then return to my
lodgings.

ARNOLPHE
Good idea. *Au revoir.*

HORACE
Au revoir. And again, *mille merci*!

ARNOLPHE
Don't mention it.

Exit, HORACE.

ARNOLPHE
   Alone. Ah, fortune! This good turn makes up for
   every trick you've played on me up to now!

*Enter HORACE, AGNES. ARNOLPHE draws the hood
of his cloak over his head, concealing his face.*

Scene 12

ARNOLPHE, HORACE, AGNES.

HORACE
Come, dear heart, no cause for alarm. I'm taking you to safety. To stay together would be suicide. Go with this good man. He will take care of everything.

ARNOLPHE, whom she does not recognize, takes her hand.

AGNES
But why are you leaving me?

HORACE
I must, dear Agnes.

AGNES
You'll come back right away?

HORACE
My yearning heart will see to that.

AGNES
Without you, life is unendurable!

HORACE
Each moment away from you is an eternity!

AGNES
If that was true you wouldn't leave.

HORACE
Only the direst circumstance drives me from you side!

AGNES
No, you don't love me as I do you. *ARNOLPHE tugs at her hand.* Why does he pull my hand?

HORACE
He only seeks to urge you on your way to safety. We cannot be seen together. He's filled with worry that we'll be discovered.

AGNES
But why should I go with this stranger?

HORACE
Don't worry, he's the only way to keep you safe.

AGNES
I'd rather stay in your hands, that's why... *To ARNOLPHE, who is tugging again.* Please stop sir, would you?

HORACE
It's almost dawn, I must go.

AGNES
When shall I see you again? *To ARNOLPHE.* Really,
sir, we'll just be a moment.

HORACE
I shall count the minutes until we are together...

AGNES
And I, too. Until then, I shall be in despair.

HORACE
Farewell! *To himself, as he goes.* Now my happiness
is assured. I fear nothing now!

Exit, HORACE.

Scene 13

ARNOLPHE, AGNES.

ARNOLPHE attempts to disguise his voice and keep his face unseen.

ARNOLPHE
Come, my child, this way. I'll take you to a place where I guarantee you won't be found.

AGNES
Is it you?

ARNOLPHE
Indeed, wicked girl!

AGNES cries out.

ARNOLPHE
I see my face gives you a fright. Is it so terrible? Clearly, my company is most unwelcome. Have I interfered in your little love story?

AGNES
Calling out. Horace!

ARNOLPHE
Too late. Don't look for help from that direction. He's too far away already. Well, well, for one so

young, how devious you are. You ask, all innocence, whether children are conceived through the air, yet you seem to have no difficulty in conceiving midnight plots to stain my honor. With what honeyed words you spoke to him just now. How did your education advance so quickly? You used to be afraid of ghosts, but I see your young gallant has taught you to love the dark. Ingrate! To deceive me so, me, who gave you everything, raised you and protected you! All the love I've shown, and this is how you repay me? Oh what a snake I have nursed at my breast and now, grown big enough, it strikes the very hand that was protecting it!

AGNES
But why are you angry with me?

ARNOLPHE
Oh, I'm unfair, am I?

AGNES
I've done nothing wrong that I know of.

ARNOLPHE
You haven't? Do you not call it wrong to run off with that young man?

AGNES
But he wants me for his wife. He told me so. I'm only following what you told me. You said that the way to avoid sin was to marry.

ARNOLPHE
Yes, but it was *me* you were supposed to marry! Did
I not make that clear?

AGNES
Yes, but if I may offer my point of view, he'd suit
me as a husband much better than you. When you
talk about married life it sounds so gloomy and
boring, but when he talks about it, it sounds so full
of rapture that I can scarcely wait!

ARNOLPHE
So you love him! You admit it!

AGNES
Of course I love him. What else?

ARNOLPHE
Have you the gall to say that to my face?

AGNES
But it's the truth. You told me to always tell the
truth.

ARNOLPHE
But how dare you fall in love with him?

AGNES
It wasn't my fault. I didn't choose to. He appeared
and before I knew it, I was in love with him.

ARNOLPHE
Then why didn't you fight those forbidden feelings?

AGNES
But why forbidden? The nuns taught me love is the highest good. Besides, all the feelings that come with it are so delightful.

ARNOLPHE
Didn't you know I would be upset?

AGNES
Why would you have anything to complain about?

ARNOLPHE
Of course! Why should I complain? I'm overjoyed at the situation! You don't love me! I couldn't be happier!

AGNES
Love you?

ARNOLPHE
Yes.

AGNES
I'm sorry, no I don't love you.

ARNOLPHE
Why not?

AGNES
You wouldn't have me lie?

ARNOLPHE
You miserable girl, why? Why?

AGNES
It's not me you should blame. He made me love him.
You could have done the same thing. I didn't prevent
you.

ARNOLPHE
I tried to make you love me with all my strength. I
did everything!

AGNES
Then I suppose he's more skilled than you. He hardly
had to try at all.

ARNOLPHE
Oh, the little peasant orphan has a quick wit now,
does she! Why no lady at court could bandy such
cruel replies with such ease. Then tell me this, since
you're suddenly such a brilliant intellect, did I raise
you all these years, at such expense, for another man
to benefit? Is that a reasonable investment?

AGNES
No, but he'll gladly repay your losses ten times over.

ARNOLPHE

How could he possibly discharge your debt to me?
It's too large.

AGNES

And yet it does not seem all that great.

ARNOLPHE

Did I not raise you from infancy?

AGNES

Yes, you did, and I'm very much obliged for the
thoroughness of my education. Do you really think I
can't see what you've done to me? I'm humiliated to
be so ignorant in even the simplest things.

ARNOLPHE

And do you think you'll learn everything you need at
the hands of that young fop?

AGNES

Yes. It's thanks to him I know the little I do now. I
already owe him much more than I do to you.

ARNOLPHE

What stops me from beating you senseless I don't
know. Your cold heart makes me ache to punish
you.

AGNES

Then beat me, if that's what you wish.

ARNOLPHE

Aside. See that? Just that? Those soft words, that falling look and my heart is wrecked, overcome with tenderness again, longing only to embrace and coddle her. How strange love is! How wrong it is that men, at the hands of such lying, willful creatures, will endure so much. Women, as everyone knows, are frail, foolish, and illogical. Their souls are weak, they have no character or discipline. There's nothing so silly, so mad, so faithless, yet what won't we do to please them, to receive a single kind look or tender word?

To AGNES. Come, little traitor, let us be at peace. I'll pardon you and love as ardently as I did before. Learn from my graciousness, and repay it by loving me in return.

AGNES

If I could, I would, but I can't.

ARNOLPHE

You can, my precious beauty, if only you'd try. *Sighs.* Just listen to that heartfelt sigh. Look at the suffering in my face. Reject that puppy and the love he offers. You'll be far happier with me. With what clothes and jewels and fineries I'll spoil you. I'll pet you day and night, and shower you with all the little goodies your heart desires. You shall have your wish in everything. Do I have to say more?

Aside. God, to what extremities desire drives us! I can't believe myself!

To AGNES. In short, sweetest girl, no man's love could be a match for mine. What more proof do you need? Tears? Blood? Shall I tear my hair out? What will convince you? Shall I kill myself? Command me anything, cruel one, and I'm ready to obey

AGNES
All this talk. Horace, in two words, would have seen me melt at his feet.

ARNOLPHE
That's it! Enough of your impudence! I won't take no for an answer, you stubborn dunce! I'll pack you off to the country! You think you can spurn me like this? You can savor your memory of this little scene locked away in a convent cell!

Enter ALAIN, GEORGETTE.

Scene 14

ARNOLPHE, AGNES, ALAIN, GEORGETTE.

ALAIN
Come quick, sir! Agnes has vanished!

GEORGETTE
We think she ran away with the corpse!

ARNOLPHE
She's right here, you idiots. Shut her away in her room and lock the doors and windows. He wouldn't have the nerve to try to come for her there, and even if he did, I only need half an hour. I'll get a carriage and we'll be off. Take her away and don't let her out of your sight!

Exit, ALAIN, GEORGETTE, with AGNES.

ARNOLPHE
Alone. Perhaps a little change of scenery will wean her away from this childish infatuation.

Enter, HORACE.

Scene 15

ARNOLPHE, HORACE.

HORACE
Monsieur Arnolphe, thank heavens you're still here!
I'm beside myself with grief. Heaven's cruelty is
unimaginable, is it not?

ARNOLPHE
I couldn't agree more. What's the trouble now?

HORACE
You would never believe it.

ARNOLPHE
Give it a try.

HORACE
It's the most vicious blow of fate you could imagine!
Despite all my good fortune up to now, at the very
last moment, my precious Agnes, my prize, will be
snatched away from me!

ARNOLPHE
How tragic. Do tell.

HORACE
It's beyond belief! My father had just arrived, and no
sooner had he embraced me than he revealed the
nature of his mysterious errand. He has made a

match for me! And whether I like it or not, I am to
be married to this girl today, this very morning! Can
you imagine my despair?

ARNOLPHE
I have a little idea.

HORACE
What blacker curse could fall on me? I told you
yesterday of Henri. It's he who is responsible for all
my new misery. He's come here with my father,
determined to wed me to his only daughter. The
cruelty of it!

ARNOLPHE
My poor, dear boy.

HORACE
And since my father said he was on his way to you
immediately, I ran ahead to warn you of my
situation. Sir, I beg of you not to let him know of
Agnes and me. He'll be furious! But since he places
such faith in your good judgment and wisdom, try
sir, try to dissuade him from this awful match. Plead
my case!

ARNOLPHE
I will do what's best, I can assure you.

HORACE
And even if you can't persuade him, at least beg him
to delay a few days. Anything to give me time.

ARNOLPHE
You can rely on me to resolve the situation entirely.

HORACE
On you my dearest hopes depend.

ARNOLPHE
Don't give it another thought.

HORACE
How wonderful a friend you are! How right my father is to hold you in such high esteem! Ah, here he comes. Allow me to give you a few arguments to try on him.

HORACE whispers to ARNOLPHE. Enter ORONTE, CHRYSALDE, HENRI.

Scene 16

ARNOLPHE, HORACE, CHRYSALDE, ORONTE,
HENRI.

HENRI
To CHRYSALDE. No need for introductions, sir. I
knew you as soon as I set eyes on you. You are the
very image of your late sister, my adored wife. How
cruel the destiny that robbed me of her, and after all
the years of hardship we bore together in that terrible
New World. If only she had lived to enjoy the good
fortune that followed her untimely death. But fate
had it otherwise. Let me then, at least, find solace in
what joys I may provide for our sole child. You, sir,
are concerned in this matter. See if you approve of
the plan I have for her. Oronte's young son is the
ideal choice, don't you think? But tell me frankly. I
consider you, speaking for her, to have an equal
voice in this.

CHRYSALDE
I've better judgment than to question such a worthy
suggestion.

ARNOLPHE
To HORACE. Yes, yes. Don't worry. I shall
represent you more truly than you expect.

HORACE
Once again, don't tell him..

ARNOLPHE
I promise.

*ARNOLPHE leaves HORACE, goes to embrace
ORONTE.*

ARNOLPHE
Ah, my old, dear friend! How are you?

ORONTE
What a warm greeting! I'm delighted to see you
again.

ARNOLPHE
How welcome you are!

ORONTE
I've come to town...

ARNOLPHE
You needn't say a word. I know what brings you.

ORONTE
You've heard already?

ARNOLPHE
Yes.

ORONTE
  Good, then.

ARNOLPHE
  However, I must tell you this. Your son looks on this
  match with dread. His heart is sick at it, in fact, he's
  begged me to plead with you to reconsider.

ORONTE
  He has?

ARNOLPHE
  Indeed. But let me share with you my opinion, if you
  don't object.

ORONTE
  Not at all. What do you advise?

ARNOLPHE
  I wouldn't think of it. Exercise a father's rights and
  insist he do as he's told. What the young need is
  discipline, friend, discipline. I'd make him tie the
  knot without a moment's delay.

HORACE
  Aside. Traitor!

CHRYSALDE
  But friends, if the match repels the boy, perhaps we
  should not insist. I'm sure my brother-in-law agrees.

ARNOLPHE
Should a man be governed by his son? For shame!
Would you have a father not insist on obedience
from his child? At his tender age of wisdom it would
be grotesque indeed to see him lead the one who
should be leading him. No, my dear friend is bound
by honor. He's given his word. Be firm, and set an
example to your son about how to fulfill one's duty
in life.

ORONTE
Well said. We should proceed with this alliance. I'll
answer for my son's consent.

CHRYSALDE
To ARNOLPHE. It much surprises me to hear you
press this marriage with such determination. What
are you up to now? I can never make you out.

ARNOLPHE
Don't worry friend, I know what I'm doing.

ORONTE
Indeed, Arnolphe...

CHRYSALDE
Please, friend, he finds the name objectionable. Do
not call him that. Address by his proper name,
"Monsieur de la Souche."

ARNOLPHE
No, no. No matter, really I...

HORACE
What's this? "Monsieur de la Souche?" You?

ARNOLPHE
You heard. Now you know. And perhaps you can finally understand why I have spoken in the way I have.

HORACE
Of all the rotten scoundrels!

Enter, GEORGETTE.

Scene 17

ARNOLPHE, HORACE, CHRYSALDE, ORONTE,
HENRI, GEORGETTE.

GEORGETTE
  Sir, come quick! We can't hold Agnes! The girl's
  gone crazy. She's frantic to escape. I think she might
  jump out of the window!

ARNOLPHE
  Bring her here. We'll put an end to this nonsense this
  minute.

Exit, GEORGETTE.

ARNOLPHE
  To HORACE. Cheer up. You've had your share of
  good luck. Remember, every dog has his day.

HORACE
  What man was ever betrayed like this? Or hurled
  into such a hopeless hell!

ARNOLPHE
  To ORONTE. Don't delay the wedding vows for an
  instant. And I'll be delighted to attend.

ORONTE
  Don't worry. We shall proceed immediately.

Scene 18

ARNOLPHE, HORACE, CHRYSALDE, ORONTE,
HENRI, ALAIN, GEORGETTE, AGNES.

Enter, ALAIN, GEORGETTE with AGNES.

ARNOLPHE
Well, my pretty child, you who are so willful and ill-behaved. Here is your young gallant. Perhaps you should curtsy as you leave. *To HORACE.* Farewell, boy. All your sweet hopes seem to have turned bitter. You understand, now perhaps, that love doesn't always conquer all.

AGNES
Horace! Will you let him take me away from you?

HORACE
Father, I beg you to reconsider!

ARNOLPHE
Come, chatterbox.

AGNES
I won't. I won't budge from this place. I'll die first.

ORONTE
Now what on earth is the mystery here? Would you kindly explain?

ARNOLPHE

Some other time. Until then. We must be on our way.

ORONTE

And where exactly do you intend to go? What's the meaning of all this?

ARNOLPHE

Don't concern yourself with my affairs. Go ahead with the wedding of your son and let me be about my business.

ORONTE

That's exactly what I intend to do. But has no one told you that the one I intend him to marry is this young woman here?

ARNOLPHE

What? Her?

ORONTE

Of course. Henri's long-lost child. The very one who has been living in your house. Now then, do you intend to explain your wild statements just now?

CHRYSALDE

I confess I too was amazed at what I heard.

ARNOLPHE

What are you all talking about? This is pure gibberish.

CHRYSALDE
My sister married secretly. Her daughter's birth was kept from the family.

ORONTE
The child was placed in the keeping an old country peasant woman who raised her under a false name.

CHRYSALDE
My sister's husband, Henri here, having lost everything, had to leave France to try his fortune in the New World.

HENRI
And undergo terrible trials and miseries in that strange land.

ORONTE
Where, through great enterprise, he managed to not just regain what he had lost through men's deceit, but multiply it many times over into a great fortune.

HENRI
Returning home, I at once sought to find the nurse with whom we had left our daughter.

ORONTE
And the good creature told him, which was the truth, that she had turned her care over to you.

HENRI
   Thinking you would be better able to care for and
   educate her.

ORONTE
   We've brought the good woman here to reward her
   and set things right at last.

HENRI
   She'll join us in a moment, and then we'll have a
   public end to this mystery.

HORACE
   Father, a great coincidence has occurred. What you,
   in your wisdom, desired, has already taken place.
   The fact is, I am bound by the deepest ties of love to
   this magnificent girl. It was she you sought, and it
   was for her sake that I opposed your will.

HENRI
   I recognized her from the first. My joy is too deep
   for words. Come here, dearest daughter.

They embrace. HENRI embraces HORACE as well.

HENRI
   My son!

ARNOLPHE cries out in speechless rage.

CHRYSALDE
   There, dear man. I know you're in a painful state of

mind, yet see that perhaps what fate has decreed might be for the best. Your chief desire in life to avoid having horns on your head. All you have to do now to prevent it is never get married! See what a close escape you've made? My congratulations!

ORONTE
And mine!

HENRI
And mine as well!

ARNOLPHE
Idiots! Buffoons!

Exit, ARNOLPHE.

ORONTE
Now why is he rushing off like that?

CHRYSALDE
Come, it's time to celebrate. Let us go in, comfort our poor dear friend Arnolphe, and rejoice that heaven orders all things for the best!

THE END

Frédérique Michel & Charles Duncombe

Frédérique Michel was born in Paris and studied theatre at the Conservatoire. She is the Artistic Director of City Garage. Charles Duncombe is a writer, producer, designer, and serves as the Managing Director and Dramaturg of the company, which they have run together in Los Angeles for over twenty-five years. They have won numerous awards for their work, including the Los Angeles Drama Critics Circle's Margaret Hartford Award for Sustained Excellence in Theatre, the Otto Rene Castillo Award in New York for Political Theater, and The "Queen of the Angels" Award from the LA Weekly for "decades of directing and producing scintillating, politically charged theater that challenges audiences to reconsider their assumptions about the nature of politics and the nature of theater itself." Their translation and adaptation of *The Marriage of Figaro* won the 2010 LA Weekly Theater Award for Best Translation.

CPSIA information can be obtained at www.ICGtesting.com
Printed in the USA
LVOW07s0811100116

469962LV00016B/139/P